GOLIA [illegible] RS

Goliath is the biggest dog for miles around, so it seems funny that his best friend is a very small dog called Nipper. One day, Nipper is stolen and a ransom note from the dognappers means the end of his owner's life-savings. David, Goliath's young owner, has a few ideas as to who the dognappers are, and he can count on Goliath for plenty of help . . .

This is the third David and Goliath adventure

About the author

After studying at Cambridge, Terrance Dicks became an advertising copy-writer, then a radio and television scriptwriter and script editor. His career as a children's author began with the *Dr Who* series and he has now written a variety of other books on subjects ranging from horror to detection.

Also by Terrance Dicks and available from Knight Books

Goliath and the Buried Treasure
Solve it with Oliver: The Mystery of the Missing Train
Ask Oliver: The Fireworks Mystery

The Adventures of
David and Goliath

GOLIATH AND THE DOGNAPPERS

Terrance Dicks

Illustrated by Valerie Littlewood

KNIGHT BOOKS
Hodder and Stoughton

First published in Great Britain by Piccadilly Press 1984

Knight Books edition 1987

British Library C.I.P.

Dicks, Terrance
Goliath and the dognappers.——
(The adventures of David and Goliath).
I. Title II. Littlewood, Valerie
III. Series
823'.914[J] PZ7

ISBN 0 340 42389 7

The characters and situations in this book are entirely imaginary and bear no relation to any real person or actual happening.

Printed and bound in Great Britain for Hodder and Stoughton Paperbacks, a division of Hodder and Stoughton Ltd., Mill Road, Dunton Green, Sevenoaks, Kent TN13 2YA.
(Editorial Office: 47 Bedford Square, London WC1B 3DP) by Cox & Wyman Ltd., Reading

CONTENTS

Chapter One

Goliath and Nipper

Goliath was the biggest dog in the street.

In fact he was the biggest dog for miles around.

David's father - David was Goliath's owner - said Goliath was probably the biggest dog in the world - and the hungriest. So it seemed funny that Goliath's best friend was a very small dog called Nipper.

Not that they started off that way.

Nipper was a Jack Russell terrier, and, although he was very small, he was very fierce.

Nipper belonged to the lady who owned the launderette at the bottom of David's street.

Goliath was fond of the launderette.

He liked to sit outside the window and watch the clothes in

the machines going round and round.

David thought Goliath probably had the idea that the washing machines were some kind of television set and he was waiting for the cartoons to start.

But one day the launderette lady bought a dog to keep her company. Since she lived by herself in a very small flat she chose a very small dog.

A Jack Russell terrier.

Right from the beginning, Nipper was determined to be a good guard dog.

At first he even tried to guard the shop from the customers, rushing at them yapping furiously when they came in with their washing. After a while, the launderette lady managed to teach Nipper that customers were friends and he let them in.

But although he allowed people in the shop, Nipper drew the line at other dogs.

He didn't even like them in the street outside.

Whenever another dog came anywhere near the launderette, Nipper would hurl himself at it, barking furiously.

The launderette lady had to put a big 'No Dogs Please' notice in the window of her shop.

The first time Goliath met Nipper was quite an occasion. Goliath was ambling down the street with David one Saturday morning. As usual, he stuck his head inside the open doorway of the launderette for a look at the machines when suddenly this tiny ball of fur hurled itself towards him, yapping loudly. For all his huge size, Goliath was actually a bit on the timid side, and he backed away.

Encouraged by this retreat, Nipper chased him out into the street, still barking.

Outside on the pavement, Goliath had time to realise that his attacker, although noisy, was really very small indeed.

Peering down at Nipper, Goliath gave a tremendous 'Woof!' that sent Nipper scuttling back into the safety of the shop.

Giving David a, 'what was all that about?' look, Goliath trotted on his way.

Immediately, Nipper, thinking

Goliath was retreating, dashed out of the shop after him, barking fiercely.

Goliath turned and barked back, and Nipper shot back inside the shop. This happened several times, until David and Goliath were far enough down the street for Nipper to feel that he'd driven them off, and honour was satisfied.

Nipper trotted back into the shop wagging his tail, an 'I showed 'em' expression on this face.

Later that afternoon when the shop was closed, David and Goliath met the launderette lady, and Nipper on the Common. David was afraid there'd be more trouble, but to his astonishment, Nipper ran up to Goliath wagging his tail, barking in quite a friendly fashion.

Goliath looked down in astonishment as Nipper began running round him in circles in an obvious invitation to play.

Delightedly, Goliath joined in the game and the two dogs rushed about chasing each other.

The launderette lady watched them, smiling broadly. 'Just look at that, then. All that fuss this morning, and now they're the best of friends!'

Later that same afternoon, Goliath stuck his head inside the launderette to say hullo to his new friend - and was very hurt when Nipper dashed out and chased him off again!

Things went on like that from then on. On neutral territory so to speak, Nipper was as friendly as could be, always pleased to see his big friend and always ready for a game. But whenever Goliath came near the shop, Nipper turned back into a fierce guard dog, and insisted on chasing him away.

Goliath got used to it eventually,

and the chasing off became a kind of game in itself, much to the amusement of the launderette lady and her customers. There was something very comic in the sight of such a tiny dog seeing off a huge animal like Goliath.

One Saturday morning a few weeks later, David and Goliath were going down the street on their way to the newsagents on the corner. David had promised his parents that he would only buy sweets one day a week, and Saturday was sweet day - one of Goliath's favourite occasions.

As they passed the launderette Goliath paused, waiting for his little friend to come out and chase him off.

Nothing happened.

Goliath gave David a puzzled look.

'Maybe he's not feeling well,' said David.

Just then the launderette lady appeared from the back of the shop. Her eyes were red, and it was obvious that she'd been crying.

'What's the matter?' asked David. 'Is Nipper ill or something?'

She shook her head. 'He's gone - disappeared?'

'You mean he's run away?'

She shook her head again.

David looked alarmed. 'You don't mean Nipper's been stolen?'

Worse than that,' said the launderette lady. 'He's been kidnapped!'

Chapter Two

The Dognapper

David stared at her. 'Kidnapped? You mean dognapped. How do you know?'

'I got this note.'

She held out a grimy scrap of paper. 'It was pushed through my door last night, a couple of hours after Nipper disappeared.'

David read the note. It said, 'WE WANT A THOUSAND POUNDS, OR YOU WILL NEVER SEE

NIPPER AGAIN. NO POLICE. ORDERS LATER'.

It was written on a grimy scrap of lined paper, and printed in pencil in big block capitals.

David studied the note for a moment. 'What will you do?'

'I don't know,' sobbed the launderette lady. 'I haven't got a thousand pounds, nothing like it. I could take my savings out of the bank but it wouldn't be nearly enough. It's not as if I could sell the shop, I only manage it, I don't own it.'

'I think you ought to go straight to the police.'

'I daren't. Suppose the dognappers are watching me? They'd see if a policeman came to the shop. And they'd see if I went to the police station.'

'You could ring them up.'

'They'd think I was just some silly old woman fussing about a lost dog.'

'I could take the note to the police station for you.'

The launderette lady shook her head. 'No, you mustn't. They might find out somehow and then I'd never see my Nipper again. I'll just have to take my savings out of the bank and hope they'll take less money.'

David nodded. 'I should think they probably will. I was reading an article about kidnappers in the papers. It said they often ask for a huge lot of money just to frighten you. Then when they bring the price down you're glad to pay. I still think you ought to go to the police, though.'

But the launderette lady insisted she didn't dare, and nothing David said could change her mind.

'All right, then,' said David determinedly. 'We'll get Nipper back for you - me and Goliath!'

Hearing his name Goliath barked enthusiastically, and wagged his tail.

'How on earth are you going to do that?'

'I don't know, but we'll manage somehow. Goliath is part bloodhound you know.'

Actually, David wasn't too sure of this. But as David's dad always said, Goliath was part everything, so there could easily be some bloodhound in there somewhere.

‘Have you got anything with Nipper’s scent on, just to give Goliath a start?’

The launderette lady found an old rolled-up sock that Nipper kept in his basket to play with. She let David keep the note, and agreed to tell him when she got the next message from the dognappers.

The lady went back inside the shop and David stood on the pavement for a moment, scratching his head.

It was all very well promising to help, but where could he begin?

Better start off by testing the bloodhound theory, thought David. He held up the sock to Goliath and said encouragingly, ‘Seek, Goliath. find Nipper!’

Goliath stared at him in

amazement.

David waved the sock under his nose. 'Go on, boy. Seek!'

Suddenly Goliath got the idea - the wrong idea. He snatched the sock from David's hand and bounded off down the road with it. Halfway down he stopped, puzzled to see that David wasn't chasing him.

‘Bring it back, you silly great thing,’ shouted David.

He ran up to Goliath - who waited till he was almost in reach of the sock, and then galloped off again, wagging his tail.

This happened several times, and David had quite a job convincing Goliath that the sock wasn’t just a toy.

So much for bloodhounds, thought David. His only other hope was the note and he studied it thoughtfully.

It didn’t seem to offer many clues.

No doubt the big block capitals were to disguise the dognapper’s handwriting. They were written in perfectly ordinary pencil, and the lined paper might have been torn from any old exercise book.

David stared hard at the note. There *was* something striking about it after all. Not because it was strange, but because it was so familiar. David filled many a page of lined paper like that himself. It was exactly the same kind used in the exercise books in David's school.

Not that that proved anything. Other schools probably used exercise books just like that, and no doubt you could buy them in lots of newsagents.

All the same it was a start. Just suppose it *was* someone in David's own school - who could it be?

David's was quite a big school, and like any other it had one or two bad characters.

But was there anyone bad enough to do anything really criminal like this?

There were boys who'd shove you over in the playground, or snatch your books and chuck them over a wall. There were boys who would let off fireworks in the street and scare old ladies, or keep ringing the bell on a bus and drive the conductor crazy . . .

No, thought David, for something as bad as that it just had to be . . .

And as if in answer to his thought, the boy he was thinking about appeared round the corner, a scruffy figure in black jeans and black sweater. Ricky!

Chapter Three

The Stakeout

Ricky was the school's one really bad character. He hardly ever did any work in class, and when he did he cheated.

He crawled round big tough kids, and tried to bully little ones. Sweets and toys and money seemed to disappear when he was around. He'd been suspected several times of taking money from people's pockets in the cloakrooms and even of stealing things from the school, but nothing had ever been proved.

Ricky was a skilled and convincing liar, and he never owned up to anything. He was a coward too, and a sneak.

Yes, decided David, if anyone in his school would stoop to dognapping it would be Ricky . . .

By now David was so convinced Ricky was guilty that he almost went up to him and demanded Nipper back - but then he stopped himself. He didn't have an atom of proof. There he was thinking of a possible criminal, and the suspect obligingly appeared. It was too good to be true . . .

Or was it, thought David suddenly.

What was Ricky doing here, anyway?

He lived quite some way away. David had never even seen Ricky in this area before, let alone in this street. Why should Ricky suddenly decide to spend a morning hanging round here?

What was he doing? Watching the shop for the dognappers, thought David. Seeing if the lady called the police.

Stuffing Nipper's sock and the dognappers note into his pockets, David knelt down to pat the puzzled Goliath, peering at Ricky from behind the shelter of the huge dog.

Ricky wasn't doing anything - just hanging about. He sat on a wall on the corner of the street and

lit a cigarette. Typical of Ricky to think it clever to smoke.

'What next?' thought David.

Goliath barked impatiently. Suddenly, David realised they hadn't paid their visit to the newsagents.

'Quite right,' he thought. 'Act natural!'

David went down the street and into the shop, carefully *not* looking at Ricky on the way.

He went into the shop and bought his sweets. A bar of chocolate and an assortment of odds and ends from the 1p tray, including a giant jelly-baby for Goliath.

Goliath loved jelly-babies. David tossed the sweet up in the air, and Goliath caught it and snapped it up.

David came out of the shop and walked back towards his house, thinking hard.

If Ricky was watching the shop, then he had to watch Ricky.

But how could he do it without being seen.

Suddenly, David had an idea.

David's family lived on the bottom two storeys of a four-storey house, and David's bedroom was on the first floor looking out onto the street.

On a shelf in his room, David had an old pair of binoculars handed down from his grandfather. They were old and battered, but they were very powerful.

David rushed up to his room, followed by a puzzled Goliath, grabbed the binoculars, opened his window at the bottom, and raised the binoculars and looked out into the street.

It was a shortish street, quite straight except for the end where it curved round like a hockey stick. The newsagents and the launderette were set into the curved bit, and David could see them perfectly.

He could see Ricky too, leaning

against the phone box on the street corner, staring intently at the launderette.

David settled down to watch.

It was a long morning.

David sat at his window, staring down the street.

Goliath lay slumped on the mat, wheezing and grunting in protest. It was a rotten Saturday morning as far as he was concerned, no Saturday morning telly and no walk either.

David's arms began to ache from the effort of holding the binoculars, and he had to put them down from time to time to take a rest.

For a long time nothing happened. Just people coming in and out of their houses, going shopping, pausing to chat . . .

The launderette lady came out of her shop, shutting the door behind her and fixing a note on it.

So powerful were the binoculars that David could even read the notice. It said, 'Back in five minutes'.

The launderette lady went off down the street - and Ricky followed her!

David watched and waited.

A quarter of an hour later, the lady came back, took the notice off her door and went back into the launderette.

A few minutes later, Ricky appeared, taking up his position by the phone box.

He seemed nervous now, and kept looking at his watch.

Suddenly he straightened up and went inside the box, shoving aside an old lady who was just about to make a call.

David leaned forward, focussing the binoculars.

To his surprise he saw that Ricky was making no attempt to use the telephone. He was just standing inside the box, looking at his watch.

David glanced at his own watch. It was just eleven o'clock.

He looked back through the binoculars and saw that Ricky suddenly snatched up the phone and began talking.

For a moment David was baffled, then he realised what was happening.

Someone was calling Ricky in the box at a pre-arranged time. Ricky spoke briefly, nodded, then put down the phone.

He waited for a few minutes longer, fished coins out of his pocket, picked up the phone and began to dial.

David watched fascinated as Ricky shoved money into the box and began reading from the scrap of paper in his hand. He spoke for a very short time, not much more than a minute David reckoned, and then slammed down the phone.

Then he left the box, letting in the indignant old lady, and took up his position on the corner.

David put down the binoculars, thinking hard.

Then he put the binoculars away and went downstairs, Goliath lolloping after him.

He found his mother in the kitchen making a cake.

David stuck his finger in the mixture and licked it.

'Get off,' said his mother. 'Here!' She finished her mixing and gave him the wooden spoon to lick clean.

David said, 'Mum, do you ever use the launderette down the road?'

'Only when my washing machine breaks down - though that's often enough, heaven knows. Why?'

'Could I take some things down for you? I've always wanted to use one of those machines.'

'Whatever for?'

'Please Mum, it's important.'

David's mother gave him a puzzled look. 'You can take that old bedspread from the spare room, that needs a wash. It's too big for my machine, but the launderette ones will take it.'

Ten minutes later, David was walking down the street towards the launderette, the bundled-up bedspread over his shoulder. Goliath at his heels.

Ricky stared at him for a

moment, and then looked away. David carried on into the shop, hoping desperately that Ricky would take him for just another customer.

The shop was empty, and as soon as she saw him, the lady came rushing over. 'I've heard from the dognappers.'

'I know,' said David. 'At eleven five exactly!'

'How did you know that?'

'Never mind for now. What did they say?'

'I'm to put the money in a plastic bag and toss it into the third wastebin on the left in the lane that leads across the Common. At one o'clock exactly. Then I'm to turn round without looking round, and come back here and wait for another call.'

'Have you got the money to give them?'

'I haven't got a thousand pounds, nothing like it. I popped out to the bank this morning and took out all my savings, just over a hundred pounds. I told the caller that was all I'd got, and he said to leave it anyway, and then they'd see.' She sighed, 'I'm just hoping they'll settle for that and bring Nipper back!'

'Let's hope so,' said David, though somehow he doubted it. Having got a hundred pounds so easily, the dognappers would probably try for more. They wouldn't give Nipper back till their victim had parted with every penny she could afford - and perhaps not even then. It would be safer for them just to dispose of Nipper and disappear.

'How did you know the dognapper had phoned?' asked the launderette lady, suddenly remembering what David had said earlier.

'I saw him.'

Before David could go on, he heard the most tremendous barking and yelling from outside.

He rushed to the shop doorway.

Ricky was flat on his back on the pavement, with Goliath pinning him down!

Chapter Four

The Giveaway

David stared at the sight in horror. He had planned on trailing Ricky, following him to wherever Nipper was hidden. But the plan, such as it was, depended on Ricky not suspecting him, not even noticing him. Fat chance of that now. You couldn't very well help noticing Goliath, not when he was sitting on top of you.

Suddenly, David realised that

Goliath wasn't actually attacking Ricky. He should have known that anyway. It was quite unlike Goliath

to attack anyone.

Goliath was playing with Ricky. It was obvious what had happened. Goliath had jumped up at Ricky with such enthusiasm that he had knocked him flat.

Ricky was thrashing about and yelling. 'Get him off! Get him away from me!' For all his tough front, Ricky was one of those people who were frightened of dogs, especially big ones.

David went over and grabbed Goliath by the collar, heaving him away. 'Come out of it, you silly great thing.'

Goliath resisted. He began running around Ricky in circles, barking. Then he stopped, sniffing eagerly at the front of Ricky's sweater.

David lugged Goliath away, and Ricky scrambled to his feet. To David's surprise, Goliath began barking at *him*, tugging at something dangling from David's pocket. It was the sock from Nipper's basket.

Suddenly David realised what Goliath was trying to tell him. He went up to Ricky and stared at the front of his scruffy black sweater. It was covered with black and white hairs!

Ricky backed away, brushing himself down. 'That dog of yours isn't safe. I'll have the police on to you!'

David decided to try a desperate gamble. 'Come on then! You can tell them about Goliath jumping up at you - and I'll tell them why he jumped - *because Nipper's scent is all over you and his hair's on the front of your sweater*. I'll tell them about the phone call you got in the box, and the call you made to the launderette lady about paying the ransom money.' David reached into his back pocket. 'I'll show them this note, with your fingerprints all over it!'

(That last bit was a bluff, but David reckoned it was worth a try.)

Ricky went pale and backed away. 'Wasn't me,' he gasped. 'It was me brother and his mates - ' He clamped his mouth shut.

Ricky's older brother was an even worse character than Ricky himself. He'd been in trouble with the police several times already.

Realising he'd given himself

away, Ricky turned about to run for it.

'Don't move!' shouted David. 'Goliath here is a trained attack dog. He caught a burglar the other day.' Ricky froze, and David lowered his voice. 'If I say 'kill' . . . Well, that'll be that.'

Actually, saying 'kill' to Goliath would have about as much effect as saying 'sausages', or any other word you could think of, but Ricky wasn't to know that.

'What do you want, then?'

'Just you come along with me,' said David. 'We're going for a little walk.'

From the doorway of her shop, the launderette lady watched in some surprise as David and Ricky and Goliath disappeared down the street.

Typical of kids, she thought. David had been so sympathetic about Nipper, so determined to help. Now it looked as though he'd just forgotten the whole thing and gone off with one of his friends. And he'd left his bedspread behind . . .

The launderette lady looked at her watch. It would soon be time to leave the money for the dognappers. She mustn't be late.

She picked up David's mother's bedspread and began putting it into one of her machines.

Chapter Five

The Ambush

It was five to one and the Common was almost deserted. There was a fisherman sitting under a green umbrella by the side of the little pond, munching his sandwiches.

Not far away, one of the keepers was picking up bits of litter with a pointed stick. An old lady with a shopping bag sat huddled on one of the benches.

The big car park opposite the pond was almost empty, except for a couple of parked cars and a small boy throwing a ball for a very big dog.

The dognappers had picked their time well. Before and after lunch, kids came on to the Common to play and grown-ups for a stroll, but for most people one o'clock itself was lunchtime, and they were at home tucking in.

At exactly one o'clock the launderette lady appeared, clutching an old plastic shopping bag. She walked down the path as far as the third of the big wire wastebins, tossed in the bag and turned and walked back.

For a long moment nothing happened.

Then a sort of shining blur appeared on the path, coming the other way. As it got nearer you could see it was a tall skinny youth, riding a bike at amazing speed.

He skidded to a halt by the bin, leaned over and snatched up the plastic bag without dismounting and was off again, pedalling back the way he had come.

A lot of things happened all at once.

One of the cars in the car park roared into life, and drove across the path, blocking the cyclist's escape.

Another car shot across the path behind him, cutting off his retreat.

The fisherman, the keeper and the old lady - now revealed as a very athletic young policewoman - all began closing in on the cyclist.

Even so, they almost lost him.

The cyclist swung his bike off of the path and began speeding across the open ground towards the car park. The bike was faster than any runner and much quicker than a car and it looked as if the fleeing cyclist would get away.

If he could reach the car park,

there was the main road and a whole network of side streets on the other side.

The cyclist scorched across the cinders of the car park - and suddenly an enormous dog leaped out from behind a car, barking loudly.

With a yell the cyclist swerved, crashed into the side of a parked van and fell to the ground half-stunned.

People came rushing up from everywhere, and soon he was surrounded.

Goliath was sniffing at the saddle bag on the fallen bike.

David went to it and opened it.

There inside, shaken but unhurt, and yapping furiously was a very indignant Jack Russell terrier -

Nipper!

Goliath barked delightedly in return, happy to have found his friend again.

The launderette lady had turned back attracted by all the commotion. She came running up, and snatched Nipper up, hugging him.

Nipper licked her face then wriggled free and jumped down. He wanted to play with Goliath.

As the two dogs chased each other round in big circles, one of the plain-clothes policemen - the one who'd pretended to be a fisherman said, 'Very clever dog, that, sonny. If it hadn't been for him, that bloke on the bike would have got away in spite of us all.'

David sighed.

It was David who'd worked out that Ricky was involved, and kept watch on him. It was David who'd marched Ricky down to the police station and made him confess, and persuaded the policemen to set up an ambush.

The capture of the dognapper - Ricky's brother's friend - had been more or less an accident. When the chase started, David grabbed Goliath by the collar and pulled him down behind a car so he wouldn't get hurt.

Goliath, convinced there was some splendid game going on, had pulled away and jumped out - just in time to scare the dognapper off his bike!

As usual, David did all the work, and Goliath got all the credit. Still, what did it matter, as long as Nipper was back safe and sound?

Nipper shot between Goliath's legs and disappeared underneath him. As usual, Goliath looked around baffled, wondering where his little friend had gone.

David looked up at the big policeman and grinned. 'Clever? Oh yes, old Goliath's a real genius,' he said. 'There's no doubt about that!'

If you have enjoyed *Goliath and the Dognappers*, you might like to read some other Knight titles:

TERRANCE DICKS

ASK OLIVER
THE FIREWORKS MYSTERY

There's nothing very unusual about the three workmen digging outside the bank. At least, that's what Oliver's gang think, and the police share their view. But for some reason Oliver just can't stop staring at them . . .

Oliver is the youngest member of Pete's gang and he and his friends have been collecting money for their guy outside the local bank. But with the sudden arrival of the men with their picks and shovels they have had to move. And it doesn't take Oliver long to become suspicious . . .

KNIGHT BOOKS

TERRANCE DICKS

SOLVE IT WITH OLIVER
THE MYSTERY OF THE MISSING TRAIN

The steam train *The African Belle* is one of the Safari Park's main attractions; that is until one evening – when not only does the last ride set off early, but it fails to come back!

Oliver and the gang help to search for the missing train, but it seems to have been spirited off into thin air . . .

See if you can solve the mystery before Oliver does!

KNIGHT BOOKS

OTFRIED PREUSSLER

THE LITTLE WITCH

The little witch was only a hundred and twenty-seven years old. That's not at all old for a witch. She spent about six hours every day doing exercises in witchcraft, but she just couldn't get her spells right. Then she got into deep disgrace at the Walpurgis Night party. She was given a year to make herself into a good witch or be expelled.

So many strange and funny things happened to her that year, she began to wonder if she would ever pass the final test . . .

KNIGHT BOOKS

OTFRIED PREUSSLER

THE LITTLE WATER-SPRITE

One spring day a little water-sprite was born in a mill pond. Like all true water-sprites he had webbed hands and green eyes and hair.

As soon as he could swim he explored the cool, green world of the pond and was even allowed to visit the world outside as long as he did not let his feet get dry!

The curious and cheeky little water-sprite had lots of adventures both in and out of the pond. Sometimes his fun and games got him into trouble, but life was always exciting.

KNIGHT BOOKS